LIFE

LIBERTY

JOY

"You only have ONE Life to live. Live it well.

You only have ONE Stage to shine on.
Shine brightly.

You only have ONE Red Carpet to Rock.
ROCK IT like a ROCK STAR!"

~ Michelle Moore Winder

DEDICATION

Thank You LORD, my God, for compelling me to write this book *before* the scamdemic began in 2020. You knew. You inspired me to lean on You for all things pertaining to life and godliness, and reminded me that YOU, ultimately, are in control.

Thank you to my life-giving, gorgeous husband, Bill. You always inspire me to be *me*- even when I might embarrass you in the process. You're my #1 cheerleader and my unwavering rock. I am so enjoying our long journey together.

Thank you to my children, Billy & Bree. Your unconditional trust and willingness to allow me to *preach* honors me more than you know. Your love for God, plus your ability to *think* and debate, lets me know that you'll succeed in whatever you put your hand to.

Thank you to my beautiful grandbabies Jayden and Colton. You never cease to amaze me with your sweet nature & brilliance. You two inspire me to fight for life, liberty & joy- for YOU, and for YOUR generation.

I LOVE you ALL!!

LIFE, LIBERTY
&
The PURSUIT Of JOY

Because Happiness is Fleeting

Michelle Moore Winder

TABLE OF CONTENTS

INTRODUCTION

They say that blood is thicker than water. But today I'm questioning who 'they' are and if they had any idea what they were talking about. I've experienced heart-breaking division in my own family, all due to truth versus lies. These past two years have added a dimension to faith that I had *no* idea existed. It began with 14 days to slow the spread, and then everything changed. Everything.

All across the US, fear seeped in like a black cloud and took over. Vision and Passion disintegrated behind the masks. Eventually division cracked the foundation of society and continues as I write this book. I pray for a better tomorrow, when corruption is conquered. Where Truth exposes the lie. A place where life, liberty and joy reign.

I'm a writer. I process through writing. I see things more clearly when I write. I'm also a reader- of God's word. I listen when He speaks and I ask Him for wisdom and clarity. And as His word says, He gives it abundantly. But sometimes it hurts to see. Sometimes, *seeing* things *clearly* brings about a challenge that we're not prepared for- or so we think.

I've always said the Lord puts me in the wrong place at the wrong time. I've seen things and heard things that are not appropriate to write about here. I've seen the depths of corruption and the depths of the pain it causes. I've seen compromise and even satanic worship. I've always warned my children and my clients, "Be very careful what you allow your eyes to see; you can't un-see things." BUT GOD...

The Lord compelled me to write this book before the scamdemic began in 2020. I had just about finished it, when He whisked me off in a new direction. He recently brought me back to it, to add another dimension and to edit what I had already written. Over the years He has completely broken my chains of fear and replaced them with complete trust in Him. I know that I won't always understand His ways, and that's a good thing. If He were only as smart as I, we'd all be in trouble....

CHAPTER 1:
Life

"Before I formed you in the womb, I knew you.

Before you were born, I set you apart." Jeremiah 1:5

As Benjamin Franklin noted, God is the AUTHOR of life. Thousands of years before scientists even began to understand the complex nature of life, scripture indicated that a baby is a human life at the point of conception. More importantly, that precious human being in the womb is endowed with a special kind of life which sets him apart from the animal kingdom. A baby has a soul from the moment of conception—

several days before he has blood—and his death will occur when his soul separates from his physical body.

It is worth noting that when Adam was brought to life by God, it was when God, unlike His creative work with the animal kingdom, breathed into Adam's nostrils the breath of life, making him a living being. That special life was granted to humans by God Himself.

LIFE. noun

The property or quality that distinguishes *living* organisms from *dead* organisms and *inanimate matter*, manifested in functions such as metabolism, growth, reproduction, and response to stimuli or adaptation to the environment originating from within the organism.

Any thinking person can read this definition of life, and realize life clearly begins at conception. Obviously, if a zygote weren't alive, it could NOT develop into a tiny baby, let alone a full grown, reasoning, adult. The definition itself establishes the fact.

So let's talk Zygotes.

> **zy·gote** (zī'gōt) definition (genetics): the diploid cell resulting from the union of a haploid spermatozoon and ovum fertilized ovum organism- a *living* thing that has the ability to act or function independently. (a fertilized egg cell)

Again, the definition itself *establishes* the fact that it is *living*. Although scientists disagree about how to define "life" in the physical sense, they all agree that a cell-whether it be the simplest cell on the planet, a blood cell, or a zygote- is alive. The chasm between a living cell and non-living matter is so immense that not only has a biogenesis never been observed to occur in nature, neither have scientists been able to artificially give life to non-living matter in a controlled laboratory. A cell is definitely alive, and provides irrefutable evidence of a supernatural Being that gave it life.

I've always found it interesting that so many fight to pass laws allowing assisted suicide, yet rarely does anyone use it. Because when it comes right down to it, we have an innate desire to *cling* to life, no matter how bad, painful, or hopeless that life happens to be. Why do you think that is? I have my theories, but for the purpose of time I'll leave them for another book.

"The fetus, though enclosed in the womb of its mother, is already a human being and it is a monstrous crime to rob it of the life which it has not yet begun to enjoy. If it seems more horrible to kill a man in his own house than in a field, because a man's house is his place of most secure refuge, it ought surely to be deemed more atrocious to destroy a fetus in the womb before it has come to light."
John Calvin

The reason I'm starting this book on life is because without life, liberty and joy don't exist. We'll leave it here for now- but I'll circle back!

CHAPTER 2:
Think

"We hold these truths to be self-evident, that all men are created equal, that they are endowed by their Creator with certain unalienable rights, that among these are Life, Liberty and the pursuit of Happiness." —

The unanimous Declaration of the thirteen United States of America. IN CONGRESS, JULY 4, 1776

SECTIONS:

- Confidence
- Thankfulness
- Forgiveness

I'll start by asking a question. One I've been asked many times over the course of my life. It's been asked by family members, by friends, by teachers, by bosses, even by total strangers. It's asked in every nation and of all ages. It's asked in every economic class & in every culture.

Are you happy?

No one has to stop and think before answering. Your answer may change in a day, a week, a month, or even in a moment. I realized years ago that happiness is completely dependent on our current situation, so is it really of any consequence? Why does it matter- if happiness is fleeting?

I've found in working with people from all different cultures that there are a lot of urban legends out there. I clearly remember finding out that what my Grandmother told me about horses lying down wasn't true. It's actually a fairly common myth. She said if a horse lies down, he's dying. I actually believed it until my daughter, a horse fanatic and owner, told me otherwise... just a few years ago. We tend to accept the myths that come from the people we love, especially if they're sincere when they teach us. Have you believed any myths in your life that you eventually realized weren't accurate? It is funny how many myths circulate from generation to generation. Some seem ridiculous, while others we're never really sure about. While many don't make a difference in our lives whether they're true or not, some, as in the horse example, can cause unnecessary problems in our lives if we believe them.

For example, we've all heard the saying, 'Time is Money' and many live their lives according to that statement, but it's simply not true. I'm here to shift the paradigm to truth. If we believe time is money, we *strive* to make more money to increase our time. Yet it actually has the opposite effect. The truth is, *time* is *life* and it is a limited resource that we cannot add to. Too many people, perhaps believing the myth, *waste* the life they have, trying to make more money. The truth is, we can *always* make more money- *especially* in this internet age- but we *cannot* gain one minute more time than we are allotted by our Creator. It's also interesting to note that while many people constantly say, "I don't have time" for this or that, others seem to find time to accomplish amazing feats. Think about it; we all have the same 24 hours in a day: 7 days a week, 52 weeks a year. Perhaps some *value* their time more than others?

While I will agree that money is important, it's the means of exchange for many of the things we need, I would argue that too many people place WAY too much emphasis on getting *more*. And the major problem with that is that they're trading *life,* and often, *peace*, to get it. I often remind my children and clients that if you chase money, money will run. Too many people think money will make them happy, but I'm here to tell you, it will NOT bring JOY.

CHAPTER 3:
Happiness Vs Joy

So, are you happy? Did you have to stop and think about it? I doubt it. BUT, is your life full of joy? That might take a hot minute to assess. It is easy to confuse joy and happiness. Many use it interchangeably- but is it? Let's look at the definition of each.

joy

noun \ ˈjȯi \

1a: the emotion evoked by well-being, success, or good fortune or by the prospect of possessing what one desires

b: the expression or exhibition of such emotion

2: a continuous state of happiness and contentment

happiness

<u>**noun**</u> hap·pi·ness | \ ˈha-pē-nəs \

1a: an instance of well-being and contentment

b: a pleasurable or satisfying experience

The root word of happiness is "Hap" which means chance.

Therefore, happiness is temporary, and fleeting. You can't really *plan* or even nail down happiness. It happens by chance depending on circumstances. You fall in love, you're happy. You break up, you're not happy. You get a raise, you're happy. You lose your job, you're not happy. You eat a carton of ice cream, you're happy. You weigh yourself in the morning... well, you get the idea.

Happiness depends on something happening. It's normally beyond your control. It doesn't last and you can't make it happen. But joy... joy is steady. It's internal.

Joy is the kind of happiness that doesn't depend on what happens. Joy is an internal state that you can learn to obtain that will REMAIN regardless of what is happening in your life. Joy is a fruit of the Spirit and cannot be taken away with circumstances.

CHAPTER 4:
Challenge Your Paradigms

I'm certain that some of you are thinking, 'who the heck does she think *she* is, challenging my paradigms?' If you're like me, you're fully invested in *your way* of thinking and you're not about to let some stranger, who calls herself an author, change your mind.

So bare with me while I give you a little background. I'm not one to boast, that would never be my purpose. Every ability and bit of knowledge I have is a gift I have received from life's trials, research and speaking to thousands of *real* people with *real* experiences, and, of course, the Lord. But I do think it's important that you know who this person is who's trying to shift your paradigms.

I'll tell you more personal stories as we get further in, (at this point, I hardly know you!) So for now, I'll stick with the most relevant info.

For as long as I can remember, I've wondered why people behave the way they do. Why their words and their actions rarely seem to be in sync. Why they would say one thing to one person and something entirely different to someone else? Why would they tell someone they love them, and then hurt them? Aside from my never-ending questions, I have an excessive curiosity for why things work the way they do. Why use this when it makes more logical sense to use that? Why do it this way? I've always longed for answers.

Even in elementary school, I *loved* Math. And yep, I wondered why girls weren't supposed to be good at Math (another myth still propagating today) when it was the ONE thing that totally made sense to me. If you did it correctly, you got the right answer. It was clear to see. Sometimes I could even figure out shortcuts to get the right answer. I love formulas. Math is just black and white, no gray area- (it's also one thing I love about the Bible.) By junior high, I excelled in Math, and it was my favorite subject. But the thing that most impressed me was that I could do it *my* way and still get the right answer. I didn't even understand the way the teacher was teaching- it made no sense to me, but if I looked at the problem on my own, I could easily figure it out.

High School was a breeze- racquetball, painting classes at the harbor or zoo, and plenty of time for socializing at the beach- as long as it wasn't *test* day. Calculus & Physics entered my life and all was great. I had a ton of friends, all my teachers loved me and were very lenient, plus, we had open campus- what's not to love?

Next thing I knew, I was in college beginning an Aerospace Engineering degree. Talk about a rude awakening. WOW! I was NOT prepared for this. My love for Math and Physics was completely drowned out by Thermo-Chem and Philosophy! WHAT is he *talking* about? I'll never forget my final in Philosophy. We spent the entire semester on Plato's Republic. None of it made any sense whatsoever to me! (*Why* would anyone *ever* need to know this stuff?) The questions were ridiculous! One I remember clearly, "when Plato says, 'the sky is blue' what is his meaning?" (Oh my gosh, who makes up this sh-t?) I know my instructor felt sorry for me and, compassionately, gave me a D. A D! I had never even SEEN a D before, much less *earned* one! I know this is a lot of detail but trust me, it's giving you insight into the way I think. I actually have a very good friend who's a Pastor who once said, "Michelle, your mind is a scary place to be." Yeah, really.

Looking back, I'm thankful I had to study more than my friends. I believe the excessive time I spent studying actually protected me to an extent. College is a very dangerous place for young women- as it was for me- but I never knew the statistics until many years later while I was doing research for my self-defense seminars. I had started a self-defense company and wanted *true* statistics so I obtained my information through the Dept. of Justice and many local detectives. (Oh what I'd give to sit down with *every* high school girl going off to college and share what I've learned.)

Due to my past, I lived in constant fear. No one knew- I was a master at hiding it with my outgoing personality. But something I've learned in working with thousands of people for over 22 years is that we *all* have a story. What I learned is that whether we remain a victim or become victorious is a choice- it's all about mindset. If we choose to focus on our past (something that *many* programs promote) we will remain a victim. We become a prisoner of our own choice.

However, if we choose to acknowledge the past, but LIVE in the present and look forward to the future, we will be victorious. A new friend, John Jubilee, says it well, referring to our pathetic past, "So what? Now what?" Studies say that 97% of people die with regrets. Be the 3%! We all have a choice in the way we spend our time... our life. We cannot blame our choices on others. They won't be with you on your death bed. We're all responsible for our choices. Including what we choose to think about. We need to constantly renew our minds. It's said that you'll be like the 10 people whom you spend the most time with. If negative friends are affecting you, get new friends. You have ONE LIFE to live- live it well.

I've learned so much throughout my years of raising children. One of the most important lessons is that life rarely does what you expect. I'll get more into this in a later chapter, but I want you to know that I'm writing this book because I sincerely want you to live the life of abundance and freedom that I live. It's your birthright and it is God's intention for you.

Although it may not sound like it now, I was completely left-brained for most of my life, something I eventually learned and worked on improving. I have always been a researcher and with the invention of the internet, I became obsessive about researching important subjects. I'll talk about balance later in the book but I'm hoping you're getting the picture. I'm not some dumb blonde who's pitching my paradigms in order to sell a book. I sincerely care about you and want you to experience joy. True joy. Unconditional joy.

To sum it up, I'm a questioner who has never been satisfied with the status quo. A researcher who delves deeply into important subjects that affect me or my loved ones. I'm an observer of human behavior, building relationships to get to the core of what's affecting that behavior. When I research, I consider the authority and what they have to gain by what they're spouting. I've been behind the scenes in investigations with the FBI and the DOJ. I am not swayed by persuasive words or impressed by man's wisdom. I am not a respecter of status or class. I am on this earth to share TRUTH and I take my purpose seriously. Yet I have a ton of fun doing it! I pray you'll finish this trip with me, and then make an informed decision about the message I share.

It's always seemed ironic to me that every person I've met who is vocal about the contradictions in the Bible has never read it. Not one book. Not one chapter. Not one verse. They hear others and they're willing to spout urban legends about what the Bible says without ever reading it. Having read it every day for

37 years (at this writing) my favorite response is, "Can you show me where it says that because I've never see it in 37 years of reading?" It's amazing that we believe myths without asking for proof. That is not me.

CHAPTER 5:
Walking on Uncharted Waters

For the past week (at least) I keep hearing the song,

> "I'm standing knee deep but I'm out where I've never been.

> Then You crash over me, I've lost control but I'm free.

> I'm going under, I'm in over my head.

> Whether I sink, whether I swim, makes no difference when

> I'm beautifully in over my head."
> By Jenn Johnson

The Lord has shown me over the past few months that in the very near future, He will reveal Himself as the God of Mt. Carmel. That He will send Fire from Heaven and change things in an instant. That He will show Himself strong to those who depend on Him and wait on Him and cling to Him. The Lord has been speaking to me for months that the coming years will be a time of abundant harvest and new birth and supernatural provision for those who trust in Him and nurture their relationship with Him. He will prove Himself as Lord of Lords and King of Kings like the world has never seen. Those who wait on Him and keep their ear to His heart will experience joy like they've never dreamed possible.

He has emphasized these Words: BREAKTHROUGH. Harvest. UNSHAKABLE. Clarity. Deeper. Wider. Higher. Further.

Prepare. Abundance. New Birth. Hope Realized. New Sound. New Day.

2018 began years of GREATER VISION. Greater Joy. Greater Reach. Greater Responsibility.

I don't take these things lightly. As I look around, I see the enemy thrashing in fear. Trying to create fear in the lives of those whose hearts are not stayed on the Lord. He KNOWS his time is short and he wants to take as many prisoners captive as possible. DON'T let him! I was recently reminded of the story of Duke Raynald III of Belgium in the 14th Century. He was a prisoner of his appetite.

Are you a prisoner of YOUR appetite? In this digitally saturated world, we have instant access to anything our minds can conceive! We are bombarded with messages of things we didn't even know exist. I often stay away from shopping because I find myself desperately needing things that I hadn't heard of, and suddenly, I know I can't possibly live without. Has that ever happened to you?

Stick close to Jesus. Meditate on His Life-giving word! Allow HIS thoughts to transform your thinking. Pray for supernatural protection for your spirit, soul and body- and for others. This is the time to get out of the boat, grab Jesus' hand and walk with Him on uncharted waters. As you cling to Him, you will be surrounded by peace & joy that surpasses all understanding.

Jesus said, "These things I have spoken to you, that in ME, you may have peace. In the world you have tribulation, but be of good cheer, I have overcome the world." John 16:33

This scripture is often taken out of context of the chapter, let alone, of the verse itself. He's been talking to HIS

DISCIPLES about leaving them, yet they'll be able to go directly to the Father. He says that He came *from* the Father *to* the world. In verse 33, He's saying if we're in HIM, we'll have peace. He has *already* overcome the world!

So let me ask you. Do you have peace? Is your trust in Jesus? Are you experiencing real joy, no matter what circumstances come your way? I'm not talking about *happiness* here. Happiness is fleeting. Everyone experiences it *sometimes,* when things are going well. What I'm talking about is when the bottom falls out and you can't make sense of the things that are happening around you. Do your peace and joy surpass your circumstances? Do you *know* that the ONE you depend on is dependable? That He will *never* leave you or forsake you? That He *always* has your best interest at heart because He is a good, good Father?

Hope is the evidence of things not yet seen. I believe that 2018/2019 will be a time of 'hope realized' to those who have waited patiently for the Lord, and continued to believe for His promises.

CHAPTER 6:
How Did I Get Here?

At this point, I want to take a few minutes to share my story. When people meet me, they often ask how (or *why*) I'm so bold about Jesus. How am I so sure He is who He says He is? To answer that, I'd like to take you back to a night that changed my life forever...

It was my final semester in college. I had just turned 21 and my roommate's boyfriend, Kevin, gave me a job at the Old Spaghetti Factory. I didn't dare tell my parents I had quit my engineering job so I would have more time to hang at the beach with my friends. I was a practicing Catholic at the time yet had a very distorted view of God. I was sure He would punish me if He knew I had made such a stupid choice.

One of my closest friends constantly invited me to *his* church, and told me he was praying I would have a *personal relationship* with Jesus. I would laugh, wondering what made this guy think God would listen to *him,* and trying to hide the fact that I didn't *want* God to notice me. I was afraid of Him.

Until one night. It was 10pm and I had just finished my shift....

CHAPTER 7:
Dark Road Home

I leaned against the old, solid wood door. Nothing. It was thick, heavy wood, but tonight it wouldn't budge. I forced all of my weight (104 pounds) against it. It suddenly gave way and I tripped through the doorway glancing down the long dark road as I caught my balance. A loud click behind me finalized my exit.

The air was balmy, heavy for a San Diego night. At the far end of the block before me a single streetlight lit up my shiny white Pinto. A chill ran up my spine. I thought I heard Kevin's voice in the distance, "I'm happy to walk you out" but, glancing back, I realized it was just a memory from my first day on the job. I shook my head, reprimanding myself for considering the ridiculous notion running through my mind. A light breeze lifted the stench of stale urine to my nostrils. My stomach churned and vomit rose in the back of my throat.

I took a few steps, remembering the time I punched a 12 year old boy who was bullying my brother. His mom called my parents after he ran home crying. No dessert that night- pretty severe discipline for a four year old. I chuckled nervously and continued walking, my Pinto clearly in sight. Uneasiness crowded me. I scolded myself for irrational fear. I considered that I had always been able to defend myself, and anyone else who needed it, then charged on, confused by my feelings.

Out of nowhere, a large image appeared from around the corner at the end of the block, not unusual for a Friday night downtown. He shuffled toward me with his hands in his pockets, watching the ground below him. My heart leaped and pounded against my eardrums. Electric hair pricked my scalp. Words echoed in my head. I imagined a voice, "Go back inside." I watched the man who didn't notice me, embedding his description in my memory: white, six four, two hundred thirty, Marine fade. Beads of liquid oozed from nervous pores as I marched on, aware of each deliberate step, as though there were powerful magnets on the soles of my shoes.

The man proceeded toward the old wooden door, never leaving the sidewalk nor glancing my way. Keeping my eyes on him, I slipped the keys from my purse and gripped the largest one tightly. High heels echoed in the silence as they methodically struck the black asphalt. I would not, could not, give in to irrational fear!

The moment we passed, he now behind me, I picked up my pace. The pounding merged to a sudden halt as I jammed my key into the lock. Immediately, I felt a dark presence behind me. A large, hot hand, wreaking as rotten fruit, gripped my neck. Swirling. Dizzy. Darkness. Black.

*****

I'm going to jump forward here- though I WILL take you back to the rest of the story. But right now, I want to share some answers to questions that many people have asked me over the years-including both atheists and Christians. It's always been interesting to me that the two groups, which seem like they should be at opposite ends of the spectrum, actually struggle with the same questions and the same struggles and the same fears.

I've been incredibly blessed to speak and coach all over the world. And what I've found is that people are the same, everywhere! No distance or age or class or cast seems to make a difference! People have the same needs; for food, clothing, shelter and love. They have the same fears; failure, loss, abandonment, sickness, death. The same desires; love, joy, peace, goodness, kindness, faithfulness...

As Solomon, the wisest man to ever live, said, "There is nothing new under the sun." I find it ironic that we think we're the most advanced generation in history. We ignore the pyramids & the incredible buildings people built years before we had automobiles and power tools. And the incredible craftsmen who carved marble and cast gold and painted frescos... I could go on, but I digress.

After working with thousands of people over the course of 22 years, I've come to the conclusion that God intended our Fathers to represent *Him*... SO, the enemy, whose passion is to steal, kill & destroy us, sends his armies to destroy the Father's relationships with their children- creating an impossible ability to trust God- not able to understand the concept of a good, good Father.

I live an amazing, abundant life of my dreams, but it wasn't always this way. I remember a time when I was afraid of everything. I had been a victim of both physical and emotional assault multiple times so I believed I was damaged goods. I adapted a victim mentality. I had given up on my dreams.

Have you given up on *your* dreams? While that's bad, the worst part is what happens next. We eventually *forget* them. We look around at other's lives and we feel powerless regarding our own circumstances. We end up watching *other's* lives and *their* accomplishments as our life subtly slips by. We can't *wait* to watch the Grammys and the Emmys and the Country Music Awards. We join the Facebook groups of our favorite gurus and pretend they're our friends. We research who our heros love, what they eat, where they hang out... We post and tweet and watch- all the while *pretending* this is *life!*

Can you relate? Have you ever felt as though others held the reigns to your life? That *your dream* is being lived by, and perhaps *intended* for someone else? Is it difficult for you to believe that *before* God formed you in your mother's womb, He *knew* you? That He has a plan and a purpose for you, for good?

This may be a good time to share the rest of the story...

I suddenly came to. I'm not sure how much time had passed. I didn't know where I was or what had taken place. Slowly, as if waking from a dream, I saw my perpetrator, standing before me, hands in the air. Mouth gaping and eyes wide open. Apparently gripped with fear, he was staring at least 3 or 4 feet above my head. I stood there, numb. Disoriented and confused, I was frozen in space and time. My legs felt like lead. Refrigeration trucks buzzed all around me, echoing in the thick, rancid air. I felt rocky dirt beneath my bare feet. My shoes and purse had vanished. My dress and nylons were ripped. Nothing made sense.

Suddenly, I felt a warm hand on my bare shoulder where my torn dress was held together by a seam. Peace ran down my body like warm oil. A deep voice behind me shouted, "RUN!" I weaved through the trucks toward the single light, my feet unaware of the rocky pavement. I continued, up the sharp asphalt, to the old wooden door. Gripping the large iron handle, I tugged. The door gave way with ease, flinging wide. I glanced back. Beyond the streetlight, stood a very tall man, dressed in bright white with a blue satin sash, holding a sword in his right hand, and I knew.

That night, over 30 years ago, I realized that the God I feared actually *knew* me and *cared* enough to *intervene* on my behalf. I committed my life to Him on my way home, alone in the car. Over time and multiple miracles, I have gained the ability to love and trust Him. More importantly, I've learned to accept His love. No turning back.

I share this story because it happened at a time in my life when I felt alone- though no one knew it. I had a ton of friends and I appeared fun, exciting & carefree. But I was afraid. I had been in constant fear for so long that I was an expert at hiding it. Everyone saw me as fun and outgoing and popular. I hid behind the thick walls I had built around myself. Walls of protection that couldn't be pierced.

Another reason I'm adding it in this book is because of the 'Me Too' movement. Below is an article I wrote for Influential People Magazine while Justice Cavanaugh was *on trial,* hoping to be confirmed. It has never been more important for our life, liberty and joy to seek truth in *all* things…

Friday, June 13, 1980. San Diego, CA. I can still smell the stench of stale urine, wafting on the warm summer breeze, from where the buildings met the sidewalks. I can hear the crackling pavement beneath my wooden heels as I ran in fear. And I can still feel his hot, sweaty hand grip my neck as I pushed the key into the car door on my shiny white Pinto. The blood draining from my head as I lost consciousness, swirling into blackness in my bright fuchsia dress...

As the crowd was cheering at Kentucky Horse Park on Saturday during the 'Thoroughbred Makeover," I received a text from my husband which said, "HE is IN!" After a week of ugly, mean-spirited, mudslinging, I knew it meant that the Senate had finally confirmed Judge Brett Kavanaugh to the Supreme Court. I squeezed my 2 month old grandson who was sweating against me while my daughter gulped down her lemonade.

To say I was relieved would be an understatement. I was thrilled. I was even elated. This wasn't about a "he said she said" and this wasn't about a man of integrity being forced to prove a negative- no, this was *much* more. This was about a law that was passed on January 22, 1973. This was about voiceless victims being delivered up to torture after being convicted of inconvenience. This was about the 43 million abortions in 2017, the majority by American women.

As I received the text from my husband, I thought about the many women I've coached whose lives were riddled with shame, guilt & sadness over their own hidden abortions and I thought about what a victory this is for women. I flashed on a day when #metoo will include women who've been victims of a billion dollar industry that thrives on death. Many of whom were also victims of sexual assault.

"What if you're me too?" That's the question I set out to ask hundreds of women long before the media lynching of Judge Kavanaugh. I wondered if my perspective, as a former victim and self defense instructor, as well as a victim's advocate, was similar to what other *real* victims felt regarding the #metoo movement and also the Confirmation hearings for Judge Brett Kavanaugh. I'll admit here that I was slightly shocked with the results. In fact, so many women felt *exactly* as I did, but that's not what surprised me most.

In working with thousands of victims of rape and domestic violence for over 22 years as an advocate, mentor and first responder,   I've heard thousands of stories, many so chilling I wouldn't even consider posting them, yet they've all touched my heart to the core. Although every story is as unique as each victim, they are all very similar in nature. One common theme is that we remember every single detail. We recall vividly, with every sense, exactly what happened.

CHAPTER 8:
Me Too

While I'm the first to say that women have a right to be heard, and encourage them to speak, I have found that *most* women don't tell of their sexual assaults. In 2015 a survey found that 82% of victims have never told *anyone.* 82%! That even surprised me, a self defense instructor, who is often the first one they tell. But what did surprise me during my survey was that, although 98% of the women I asked agreed with me, 96% were not willing to state their opinions publicly- or even in a small group of friends.

The #MeToo Movement began as a way for women to *come out,* so to speak, and share their stories of sexual assault. But it quickly turned into an open accusation forum where *any woman* could make baseless accusations in order to justify her bad choices, or visible consequences. I've met with countless women who admit to having used their sexuality to gain status, jobs, promotions, relationships, etc. and others whom have actually reported a rape to cover up their embarrassment or to be vindictive when a relationship didn't turn out the way they wanted. We've all made mistakes, but isn't it time for us to own up and stop blaming others for our bad choices? In fact, the Ms. Ford's of the world can easily be coached & paid to perform a believable testimony, but *real* victims don't want to come forward. If they do, their testimonies are clearly *not* rehearsed. They relive it over and over and you can sense it in their testimony.

No. This confirmation hearing was not about a victim and a predator. This was about *Roe vs Wade* being overturned.

Science now clearly proves that personhood begins at conception & should therefore be protected by the Constitution. It also clearly proves that babies in the womb feel pain.

Today is the day. Now is the time to overturn *Roe vs Wade*, as even Roe herself fought for.

Due to improvements in technology & Fetal Ultrasound in the early 90's, Norma L. McCorvey became pro-life in 1995, and from then until her death in 2017, she was a vocal opponent of abortion.

Congratulations and apologies to Justice Kavanaugh. You are about to make history.

CHAPTER 9:
Hurricane

Being a worship leader for many years I've had the privilege, and the curse, of being on the *inside.* It took me a while to understand that people are people- whatever their position in life. I used to live in a dreamland believing that people in authority, *especially* in a place like a church, would have higher standards for themselves; hold themselves to a higher accountability. I figured, minimum, they would be accountable to each other. Not so. Bottom line, the Bible is always right. Pride goes before a fall. And people in authority, whether it be over a nation, a business or, yes, even a church, often become hostage to pride. Of course there are exceptions, (my current Pastor being one) but that gigantic monster of pride is a tough one to keep at bay. It swallows up unsuspecting men and in the process, many innocent seekers.

In 2001, after returning from a life-changing trip to Israel, I found myself right in the center of a demonic plot aimed at destroying lives. I won't go into details as I don't believe that would benefit anyone, but I will say that it was one of the most instrumental lessons of my spiritual life. I was faced with a choice. I could drink the Kool-Aid and continue pursuing my passion for worship. Or, I could honor God and loose one of the most important things in my life. To me it was a no-brainer. But remember earlier in the book, I LOVE black and white. That is the way God designed me. Unfortunately, and much to my dismay, *most* of the people involved loved the gray area- and some even chose the black side. (Trust me, I'm getting to my point)

Things got so out of hand, people of integrity were suddenly choosing to lie rather than lose their jobs. My mind wasn't able to comprehend those things at the time. (I'm *much* wiser now.) I couldn't sleep for months. Bill & I were doing everything in our power to protect our kids from knowing what was going on- but it was so far reaching, it was nearly impossible. One night, experiencing true depression for the first time in my life, I was ready to give up. I was afraid of the way I was feeling, as I knew it wasn't me, but I couldn't even bring myself to pray. I was all prayed out and I just didn't care what happened next. I could never understand depression and I would tell people who talked about ending their lives to just hitchhike through Europe or go skydiving. Do all the things they'd been afraid of.

So at 3am, while lying there, contemplating what I should do, I suddenly felt swirling around me. I had a sense that I was in the middle of a hurricane and I could hear shrieks and screams and I saw hands reaching out to pull me in. Swirling faster and faster I was dizzy. Then I heard the Lord's voice. Clearly. Audibly. He said, "Look Up!" I looked up, and I saw clear, bright, blue, calm sky. I was drenched in a supernatural peace which I had never experienced before. It totally encompassed me. I felt warm and calm and safe for the first time ever. Then I heard Him say, "You are in the eye of a hurricane. If you keep looking around, you'll be sucked in. Look Up! I am peace. I am joy. I am always here. I will never leave you or forsake you. I never change."

By this point in my life, God had already proven Himself to me multiple times in multiple, miraculous ways. But this was one of those, forever life altering moments, which I will never ever forget. He removed a lot of my fear that night and I have never been the same. I'll admit, I didn't learn the lesson completely until much later, but I know it was instrumental in what was to come. I'm so grateful for the entire situation which my good, good Father has used multiple times in my life to teach me to trust Him. As I've often said, I wouldn't wish it on my worst enemy, but I wouldn't trade it for all the money in the world.

CHAPTER 10:
Liberty &
The Abundant Life

This morning I got a call from my daughter who's living on our Family Ranch in Kentucky. (That's a story in itself.) The water troughs were completely frozen- and she didn't know what to do! We're city girls- from San Diego, California. We've never had animals, let alone ICE!! I immediately started googling and realized this was a common problem in much of the country. I discovered that the cows drink 1 to 2 gallons per pound per day. I started doing the math and realized she couldn't possibly water them one small bucket at a time as she was doing. My research was clear that, without enough water, they would die. To add to our concern, 5 of the Mamas were pregnant! I continued to research until I realized she had to use an axe to break up the thick ice on top, then remove the large chunks of ice so the animals could drink.

I'm blown away by the wisdom of God. He had been showing me that everyone has a layer of ice on their heart. They come in varying degrees- some are thin enough for a little warmth to break through. Others need a lot of warmth to melt the thickening layer. Yet others, as *I* was, have a layer so thick that the only way to bring life is to chop it up with an axe, then gently remove the pieces to expose the life flow beneath. And there must be follow-up, warmth and care, or the cold, outside world will just freeze another layer on top!

We're all born with an innate desire to trust. That is who God made us. He wants us to trust Him. But very early on, way too soon for most, we begin to learn that we can't depend on those whose care we're under. Research indicates that, by the time were seven, most of us come to the conclusion that we're all alone in the world. That *realization*, though not true, manifests in many different ways which affect every aspect of our forming personalities. We've all heard of the different personality *types:* A, B, or C.

For my purposes here, I want to focus on Type A; the over achiever. He/she is the one who wants to do everything right and efficiently, and is willing to do whatever it takes to *achieve*. The Type A is competitive and overly ambitious and *needs* to excel. Unfortunately, that comes with a lot of stress when the end result isn't achieved.

We are born with an innate desire for liberty- to live an abundant life. While I won't get into the politics of why our system does not teach us about money, I want to bring up the point that most people have no clue when it comes to their finances. We all need money to live. The fear of 'not having enough' is a real fear. Yet it often leads to a means of compromise and/or outright sin. In a desire to get rich, many will try to take shortcuts. This is evidenced by an epidemic of gamblers and other addictive behavior as this deep desire for abundance is not fulfilled. They'll seek the *gurus* in the world system, not realizing *they* are the means by which the gurus get rich! All the while, the answer, as *always,*is in God's word.

3 STEPS to FREEDOM from DEBT

1. Tithe *Proverbs 3:9-10; Malachi 3:10-12*
2. Live Within Your Means *Hebrews 13:5*
3. Pay Your Debts *Psalm 37:21*
4. ASK GOD! *James 4: 2-3*

The truth is, it's not so much that people want *riches,* as it is that they want *liberty,* aka *freedom* to do whatever they want, whenever they want, with whomever they want. Face it, many jobs are just a form of acceptable slavery. When you're in debt- you're a slave to the credit holder. But God created us to be FREE! And He tells us the way to do it in His word! Deuteronomy 28: 1-14.

CHAPTER 11:
How Long?

I recently returned from a 3 week trip to our new Horse Ranch in Kentucky. The story of how we ended up with it is a miracle in itself which I'll share later in the book. But this story is not that. Through a stream of events, our horse-fanatic daughter and son-in-law live on the property and are learning to care for 17 cows and 4 Llamas along with their horses and 2 dogs.

My husband, Bill, and I weren't able to be there for the closing so we went out as soon as we could. January. Not a time I would suggest for people born and raised in sunny SoCal, who think 65 is FREEZING! Aubrey & Brandon were in Lexington for a year & had been at the ranch a few months. They took to *farming* quickly. We were quite impressed with their adaptability and work ethic. Brandon works a long, physical, day as a mechanic, then comes home for dinner and a physical job in front of him. Aubrey, newly pregnant and very sick, still cares for all the animals during the day. Another funny story for another time.

Bill and I arrived during the biggest storm Lexington, Kentucky's had in years. It was 6 degrees when we got off the plane and I had one of those down coats that fit in a little sack. Yeah, it was actually in my purse. In my defense, San Diego was 78 degrees when we left, so ANY down coat seemed like it would be too hot.

The ground was covered in a beautiful, glistening blanket of snow and everything in sight was frozen. The long, steep, rocky driveway up to the farm was a little sketchy- even in a 4WD truck. The typical job of feeding and trying to water the animals (all their automatic waterers were frozen) was a daunting task for a couple of SoCal kids. In my research, I found that cows drink 2 gallons per pound, which was WAY too much to give them in buckets from the house. To top it off, 5 of the cows were *very* pregnant, which meant they needed e*xtra* water. We also heard, (could be an ole wives' tale) that they give birth on the coldest days.

Our first night at the Ranch, while sound asleep, I startled awake to banging and voices and slamming doors. I threw on my sweats and ran in to the living room where my daughter was staring out the window into the pitch black night. She jumped as I came up behind her and asked,

"What in the heck is going on? It's 3:40 in the morning?"

"We heard coyotes, so Brandon went out with his gun!" she replied.

Being a Southern Californian, I was a little shocked that my dog-loving daughter would even *think* about shooting a coyote. She went on to explain that the Mamas are about to give birth so the coyotes circle to kill the babies as they're born.

I thought, "WHAT??!! Oh man, this 'Ranchers Life' is NOT for me!"

I knew Brandon had to be up at 6 for work. He came in a few minutes later, telling us that he scared the coyotes away and the cows were all safe.

I went back to bed, but couldn't sleep. I prayed for Brandon and our pregnant daughter that they would get the rest they needed, and for the cows that God would supernaturally protect them and their offspring.

The next night, just after midnight, I woke to the howling and yelping of, what sounded like, hundreds of coyotes! I'm certain it was just a pack, but in the dark of night it was pretty terrifying. But this time, the house was silent. There was no banging or shouting going on. Obviously my daughter and son-in-law were exhausted from their new life and sleeping through it. I had a choice. I could wake them, so Brandon could go out and shoot at the coyotes, or I could pray that our good, good Father would protect the cows and we could all sleep. Yes, I knew where the guns were, and yes, I'm a pretty good shot, but there was NO way in the world I could actually shoot at a living thing that was just trying to feed himself... I'm sure I'll grow accustomed to this new way of life, but I'm not there yet!

I chose to pray, and let the kids sleep. But my active mind kept picturing a cow giving birth (something I've never actually seen) and a coyote trying to rip the baby from the womb. (Am I demented?) Anyway, the howling stopped and I eventually fell asleep.

In the morning I asked the kids if they heard the coyotes around midnight, to which they both replied, "*You* know where the gun is!"

For the following three nights, I was awakened by the eerie howling and yelping during the wee hours of the moon lit night. Each time, I chose to pray, rather than wake my exhausted family, but I would lie there with horrendous pictures in my mind. The fourth night, I clearly heard the Lord ask me how long it would take me to believe.

I asked His forgiveness, and slept the rest of the trip. I don't know if there were coyotes or not, but I never heard another howl- nor did anyone else in the house. The day after we left, the first calf was born. First time Mama didn't appear to have any problems as the baby was in the pasture near the house first thing in the morning. Both Mama and Baby are Beautiful and healthy.

I realize that many of you are questioning how I clearly heard the Lord. Unless you know me personally, you aren't aware of my journey from fear to peace and from stress to joy. I'll share stories and highlights, throughout the rest of this book, about this incredible journey that has enabled me to hear God in a noisy world. And I'll show you how you can too!

One of the many awesome things about God is, your belief in Him, or not, does not in any way affect His Majestic Power or how much He loves you. In fact, if you *don't* know Him or believe He exists, He relentlessly pursues you- as a lover would. I guarantee that once you come to realize He is real, alive and well, you'll look back and easily see the times He, personally, intervened on your behalf. And you will see that He is a good, good Father.

Bill & I teach a class at local churches called, "Hearing God in a Noisy World." We teach, through the Word, Worship and Prayer, how any believer can be trained to hear God's voice... the voice of our Shepherd. Remember, Jesus said, "My sheep hear My voice, and I know them, and they follow Me;" John 10:27 and again, "I have other sheep... and they too will listen to My voice," John 10:14-16. But I'll confess right here- all that's been going on in the physical realm regarding our animals and the coyotes has been God speaking *clearly* about what's going on in the Spiritual... and I almost missed it!! He actually sent a friend to speak a prophetic word, more about her later, to slap me upside the head! (so to speak.) It was SO obvious, once I knew it; I can't *imagine* how I missed it!!

CHAPTER 12:
It's Not All About Me

December 20, 2005. I had been training for my 3rd degree Black Belt. I was in the best shape of my life- able to pump out a mind-boggling 150 *man style* push-ups every single *early* morning. I was eating clean, got plenty of rest, and was very happy with my life. But that morning, five days before Christmas, I didn't want to get out of bed. Now I realize that may not sound odd to many of you, but I *never* slept past 6! Even in college when my roommates kept me out until 2am. I've always been an early riser. That particular day, I didn't feel bad. I just felt like staying in bed. The kids, in Junior High and High School, were off for Christmas break so I didn't need to make lunches or drive or really do anything at all. My presents were all purchased and wrapped, so I stayed in bed... all day. And the next. I didn't even have to get up as I had no appetite. By day 3, I had a slight fever so figured it was the flu. Funny, I had had a flu shot about a week earlier.

On Christmas Eve, I couldn't bring myself to get up and get ready for our traditional Christmas Eve Service. Christmas day I sent off Bill & Billy to my sister's house for the big Moore Family gathering, but little Aubrey said she wasn't feeling well and wanted to stay home with me. It didn't occur to me at the time that I had freaked out my family and they were all worried about me. The last time I could remember being sick was in 8th grade. I had the flu for about 5 days and that was it. By New Years Day, 2006.

CHAPTER 13: Back to Life

I know I've said it before, but it bears repeating; I value life. Perhaps it's due to my very close call with death at 21, and my physical death on January 6, 2006, but I'd like to think that I would value life even if that weren't the case. I am a person who loves the *science* of things, *not* because it proves anything to me, but because it *confirms* the word of God for all those skeptics out there. I can always count on the fact that God's word is true, so if anyone doesn't believe something it says, I just tell them to write it down and wait it out. Science will, eventually, prove whatever miraculous concept they are doubting. I've seen it time and time again.

In addition to convincing others, as I study science, and the different functions of the way things work, I am always awed by how truly miraculous everything about life is. It encourages me in the hope that God, STILL, can do all things. That the Designer and Creator of such incredibly complex systems is certainly able to deal with the small details interrupting a life of love, joy and peace without even lifting His little finger.

New science even proves that trees and plants have their own set of organ-like functions. According to a study in Denmark in 2019, trees actually have a certain *beat* within them, similar to a human heartbeat. These researchers used advanced monitoring techniques known as *terrestrial laser scanning* to survey the movement of twenty two different types of trees. The results shocked everyone and revealed that trees have a beat pulsating throughout their body just as humans and other living creatures do. These pulses effectively do the same job in keeping rhythm and pumping liquids around the organism as a human heart pumps blood. It has long been assumed that trees distribute water via osmosis but this new research indicates a much more complex system than anyone has ever imagined.

This same research also revealed that trees move a lot during the night. Many species drop their leaves down up to ten centimeters after the sun goes down. When trees do this, it's actually because they're sleeping.

This is just one of the many new discoveries made using our ever-advancing technology. It steadies me in the truth of God's word, and allows me to believe that 'even the rocks cry out' (Luke 19:40) without questioning.

It seems that every day there is new research indicating that God's word is true, and that the complexity of nature not only indicates, but proves, that there is a brilliant, supernatural Designer behind it all. But nothing in this universe can compare to the very complex system we call *human life.*

There is proof from the first moment of attraction between a man and a woman, to the complementary anatomical structures and organs that work seamlessly together. Proof from the millions of interactions that happen on the physical, hormonal and emotional levels, to the love and pleasure of two people becoming one flesh as mentioned in Genesis 2:24 as well as in Mathew, Mark, Ephesians and 28 other Bible verses. Proof from cells, that are smaller than the head of a pin, contributing 1.5 billion letters of DNA each in order to form a new 3 billion-letter blueprint. Proof from the nonstop application of that genome as it rapidly develops into over 20 trillion cells and 200 types of tissue and hundreds of organs and meters of blood vessels all interacting together until that final moment a fully functioning, crying, squirming baby emerges from its Mother's womb 6,480 hours later.

The miracle of LIFE: The intricate, complex systems that had to simultaneously take place in order for you to be here, reading this, at this moment in time.

I love science, because it makes it impossible for the skeptic NOT to believe in a Supernatural Designer and Creator.

Although many try to deny the existence of a God of order by attempting to confuse His design, as in a change gender, they are ultimately doomed to failure. The essential sexual dimorphism is embedded in every part of the creation. In each of us, our maleness or femaleness is unchangeably stamped on over 50 trillion of our cells.

But nothing proves that we were created by a God of order better than our conscience. Human beings born after the resurrection of Christ all possess innate moral knowledge, proving the truth of God's word that "the requirements of the law are written on our hearts, our consciences also bearing witness." Romans 2:15

And of course, aligning with that is this: "For since the creation of the world His invisible *attributes* are clearly seen, being understood by the things that are made, *even* His eternal power and Godhead, so that they are without excuse. Romans 1:20

... without excuse.

CHAPTER 14:
A New Chapter

It is now March of 2022 and I stepped in to edit this book which I thought was complete. Somehow, over the past two, unprecedented, years, (which I call a *scamdemic*) I got a little distracted from getting this done. Have *you* been distracted lately? Have you allowed corruption all around you to hijack your beautiful life? As I add this chapter to my book, I ask you to hang in here and I will give you practical strategies to get back to the life you once loved... or to take hold of the *good life* you were born to live, which you may not have discovered yet! There *are* simple ways to live in peace in the midst of a raging storm. While it may not be easy- I'm confident that you can do it by following simple steps.

In March of 2020, as I saw what was happening, I mentioned to my clients, from all over the world in my Private Facebook group, that this was NOT about a virus. I mentioned that this was a planned strategy that was mainly about child trafficking, depopulation and a New World Order.

At that point, I had never been so slammed with questions & comments- and it led me to entirely change my focus from business strategies to personal strategies. Little did I know that it would last more than the promised, "14 Days to slow the spread." Here I am, over 2 years later, still educating people online how to pursue true Life, Liberty & Joy. I'll post the lessons here which my clients have paid a lot of money for. I know, if we want our sanity back as a nation, it's important to share truth with as many people as possible.

Most of my writings here have been published in multiple magazines including *Influential People, Celebrity Parents, Entrepreneur* and others.

Although I wrote this first article for couples, most of it equally applies to any relationship including those of Parent/Child or friends.

5 THINGS THAT COUPLES DO TO ENSURE HAPPINESS:

1) COMMUNICATE. Early in the relationship you trust each other- or you wouldn't (shouldn't) stay together. The sooner in your relationship you practice sharing your heart, your desires, & your non-negotiables, the happier you'll be. Unmet expectations are a major cause of broken relationships so the earlier you start sharing, the happier you'll be.

2) MOVE. Most couples live near family & friends- & sometimes it's one-sided. Take a year or two to establish your relationship in a NEW place- somewhere you both agree on that you've always wanted to visit. You'll avoid resentment and unwanted advice. It's the perfect time, before children enter the picture. You'll learn more about each other than you would in your old environment, and everything will be an adventure together!

3) START A HOBBY TOGETHER. You obviously have something in common with this person- find something you can do together on a regular basis that will be new for both of you! Learn & Enjoy Together. Change it up every 10 years or so. It keeps the excitement in the relationship. (Hike, Sail, Tango, Pottery; the ideas are endless)

4) WATCH YOUR WORDS! I can't emphasize this enough. Words hurt. Words wound. Words can destroy relationships faster than anything else. AND words can build relationships. Everyone disagrees sometimes. Everyone fights. But you can NOT take back your words so be very careful about how you yield them in an argument. Choose words that build trust, devotion & confidence with your partner. Always remember, you're in this together. And never, ever use the D-word.

5) PRAY TOGETHER. Start a habit early in the relationship of praying for each other. It's impossible to stay mad at someone when they're praying for you. YOU pray first, and remember #4... WATCH your

WORDS! And NEVER go to bed angry.

The past two years under the Covid Dictatorship has caused a struggle for many financially. Many of you have been laid off your job, others have shut down the family business. Others have had a tough time remaining afloat. But there has never been a better time to unleash the entrepreneur within you. Whether you'd like to try something new, make a hobby into a living, or simply learning to work remotely, I'm here for you. Below are a couple of articles I wrote that were published in multiple business magazines, in order to help you do just that!

7 TIPS to INCREASE PRODUCTIVITY while WORKING from HOME

Due to our changing environment, more people than ever are working from home. If there is any *good* news about Covid, there is a lot of research which indicates remote workers are more productive than on-site workers. The benefits are staggering, including no boring commute, dressing more comfortably, and no one lurching over your shoulder. Yet Loneliness, time management, and tech issues are just some of the problems you may face if you work from home.

Get a jump on it! Address the issues head on and savor the time you'll save with these **7 TIPS:**

1. SET UP and UPGRADE YOUR TECH

Tech issues can be a major problem for those working from home. Everything from internet speed & strength, unreliable internet connection, low-quality video calls to software programs that aren't tailored to your needs can make the best intentions fail. If you're not tech savvy, ADMIT it, and hire a pro- BEFORE you start!

2. SET A SCHEDULE

While it's tempting to sleep in, time management (or lack thereof) will destroy your greatest attempts to work from home. The good news is, you can start at 10AM every day. Just be sure to set a schedule and stick to it. It's important to schedule in meals, breaks, & even time to play with the dog or take a walk outside.

3. SET ASIDE DISTRACTIONS

Before you even open your computer, create a space in your home for your office. It doesn't have to be big or fancy, just make sure it allows you to focus & create. If you have an issue with food, don't set up at the kitchen counter. If you love soap operas, make sure there isn't a TV in your space.

4. SET YOUR PHONE ON 'DO NOT DISTURB'

Structure your call time appropriately. Set a schedule with supervisors, team members & clients (NOT friends!) Unless your job depends on incoming calls, place your phone on 'do not disturb' outside of your scheduled time. Let your family & friends know, you're working.

5. **SET SOCIAL TIMES**

   Working at home can be lonely so schedule in some social, work related times. Make a reservation to work one or two days a week at a local 'Co-Working, Create Space' or invite a Co-Worker to work at your home with you one day per week. Schedule a quarterly ZOOM call with your team.

6. **SET GOALS & REWARDS**

   There won't be any 'atta-boys' at home, so set tough goals with specific rewards, then follow through. Take a 3 day weekend if you finish a project early. Buy a new pair of shoes. The possibilities are endless. Just be sure to make the reward compatible with the goal. (ie, NOT a trip to Paris for getting up on time)

7. **BE FLEXIBLE & ENJOY**

Contrary to popular belief, remote workers are more likely to *over*work than slack off. When your personal and work life are under the same roof, it's harder to switch off. If you don't have a dedicated office, put your laptop out of sight when work has ended to help avoid the temptation to log back on. Enjoy the benefits of working at home. Stick to your schedule 90% of the time- and ENJOY your freedom the other 10%.

Here's a great article for those who want to get more eyes on their current business, or turn a hobby or passion into a business.

5 SECRETS to Getting BOOKED on Radio or TV

1. Find a Trending Topic you're an Expert on. It's easy to get the attention of major media if you can connect your expertise with a trending HOT topic. Be yourself. Don't try to be someone you're not- people will see right through it. Your uniqueness makes you relatable to the audience.

2. Why You? Why Now? What's the Big Idea? In short sentences state who you are & why they should care. What is your great idea or solution?

3. Keep it Short. People have very short attention spans. Speak in short, memorable sound bites.

4. Tell a Personal Story. "Facts tell, stories sell." Make your points in your story. Emotionally connect with your audience using laughter, tears, even fear. Work your credentials into your story. No one likes a braggart but you need your audience to trust you.

5. Have a Professional Sizzle Reel: Showcase your personality & expertise. A sizzle reel should be one or two minutes max, and should present you as an authority who connects easily with an audience. Be sure to use your "as seen on" logos.

And always remember, media needs you more than you need them. Offer your expertise in a professional yet relatable manner & your name will get out there. Then they'll come looking for you!

CHAPTER 15:
BRINGING IT HOME

"But the fruit of the Spirit is love, joy, peace, longsuffering, kindness, goodness, faithfulness, gentleness, self-control.

Against such there is no law." Galatians *5:22-23*

I have traveled the world consulting businesses and helping victims. What I've come to understand in the process is that, at our core, we're all the same. Whatever race, class, gender or caste system, we all desire to be loved and valued. As I've spoken to many elderly people, close to death, the majority have regrets for something they had a passion to do but never did. Rarely do they regret something they *did* do. I always tell my clients, "as long as you have breath, it's not too late to live your purpose."

Hopefully by now you realize you are an incredible, unique, miraculous human being who was *designed* by your Creator for a specific purpose. He also gives us *passion* as the engine to fire up & drive our purpose. Nothing happens by chance. The fact that you're reading this book is not coincidence. Everything in your life is the result of accumulative decisions.

Every one of us makes mistakes. The difference between the successful and the hopeless, is that the successful *learn* from their mistakes and count them as an expensive education, determined never to make the same mistake again. The hopeless tend to blame others while they throw themselves a pity party of one. Which camp are *you* in? It's never too late to switch sides. Using the information in this book, you can make the rest of your life, the best of your life. No regrets.

STILL STRIVING for MONEY??

Is your biggest challenge in life money related? Do you worry about how you're going to pay your rent or send your kids to college? Do you stress about how you'll pay for that desperately needed vacation? Is it affecting your relationships? Your Health? Your Freedom? Your Joy?

Therefore do not worry, saying, 'What shall we eat?' or 'What shall we drink?' or 'What shall we wear?' For after all these things the Gentiles seek. For your heavenly Father knows that you need all these things. But seek first the kingdom of God and His righteousness, and all these things shall be added to you. Therefore do not worry about tomorrow, for tomorrow will worry about its own things. Matthew 6:31-34

CHAPTER 16: NEVER GIVE UP on your DREAMS!

Welcome to the future! We are living in a world of complicated tech, social media and Artificial Intelligence (AI). A few years ago, I had the pleasure of being coached by Randi Zuckerberg- the brain behind Facebook's brilliant marketing campaigns and inventor of FB LIVE! (You might know her brother, Mark =) When she became a mom, her entire paradigm shifted as she pondered the world her children would be born into. She wrote a book called, "Dot Compliated" which I highly recommend. She discusses how technology and social media influence and inform our lives online and off. She provides insightful advice about technology and its impact on children and families, dating and romantic relationships, work and on one's personal identity.

Our world is changing at an exponential rate and we can no longer do things the way our parents did. No longer does it make sense to get a "J O B" and work hard until we retire. Fact is, MOST people won't have *nearly* enough money to retire in this economy from working a J O B. That's the bad news. The GOOD news is, we live in an age of instant access, where technology puts everything you need, right at your fingertips. You no longer need to travel to find and reach your buyer. Gone are the days where you peddle your goods on a street corner or advertise on

Freeway Billboard signs. While you may need to take precautions that didn't exist for our parent's generation, there is an ENTREPRENEUR inside of you just *waiting* to be set free!

If you don't currently have *at least* $10k (USD) in savings, you need to STOP what you're doing immediately! Recognize that your current "J-O-B" is NOT working. Only YOU are working. It's time to pursue that DREAM you were born with, that PASSION deep inside you, that PURPOSE you were designed for by your Creator. You've spent YEARS working HARD for your MONEY- Isn't it time to make your MONEY WORK HARD for YOU??

7 SIMPLE STEPS TO JOY

Steps you take TODAY will CHANGE your TOMORROW:

1. GO to a beautiful, quiet place, that's relaxing, preferably outdoors. Preferably barefoot. If possible, near water.

2. Worship God. REFLECT on your best, most memorable, times in life. Times when you felt you could conquer the world! Write them down and look for a pattern. What did you dream of becoming when you were young? What were your secret desires?

3. Talk to God. FOCUS on what you want for your life. *(Do NOT pay attention to what you don't*

want.) WHY do you want it? Go DEEP! Keep asking yourself WHY until you get to the deepest core of your desire.

4. Now ask God what *He* wants for you. DO NOT WORRY about the HOW- it will come automatically!

5. CHANGE your NEGATIVE EXPECTATIONS!! *(Be honest. When you read #4, what was your self-talk? Was it positive? Or negative?)* Remember He is a loving Father who wants your *best* for you.

6. CHANGE your NEGATIVE EXPECTATIONS!! *(it bears repeating!)* BELIEVE!

7. EXPECT IT! ACCEPT IT! Convince yourself you've ALREADY attained it! Thank God, often... for everything! "Oh give thanks to the Lord for He is good and His mercy endures forever." Psalm 136:1

Don't waste another minute!! Start working on this shift in mindset TODAY, during the end of the lockdown so you can CHARGE out of the STARTING GATES when this scamdemic is over! Leave the competition in the dust. Restore Relationships. Follow your PASSION & the MONEY will COME.

You're already well on your way to achieving Life, Liberty and the Pursuit of Joy. If you're reading this, you have Life. Liberty is about choice. As Paul said when he was in prison,

"Where the Spirit of the Lord is, there is freedom." 2 Corinthians 3:17

Are you experiencing true freedom? The freedom to make decisions without restraint, and the ability to act without control or interference? According to the scripture above, freedom is an attribute of a life with God. Stepping into the presence of the "Spirit of the Lord" begins with a simple confession:

> "Lord, I am a sinner. I'm sorry for sinning against You and breaking Your heart. Thank You for dying on the cross for my sins. I receive Your free gift of eternal life and I turn from my past as I commit to following You. Teach me Your ways. Thank You for forgiveness, in Jesus mighty name, Amen."

Freedom is mandatory if you want to have joy. It's abundantly clear that our nation's founders understood that. The pursuit of Joy comes from *true* wealth. True wealth only exists where there is a healthy balance in your life of relationships, health, finances, and yes, freedom. Anyone can attain this balance. And while it may not be easy, it *is* simple. You see, dear reader, joy is a *fruit* of the Spirit of God living in you. You cannot attain it in any other way. Just as an apple is the fruit of an apple tree, and just as grapes are the fruit of a grapevine. Joy only grows as you're planted and grounded and well watered in God's garden. And of course you need to bask in the light of the Son and allow it to shine right through you. That is how you pursue Joy.

This brings us full circle back to LIFE.

Life is short- and unpredictable as we've discovered. Take it by the reigns and direct where *you* would like it to go.

*Therefore we also, since we are surrounded by so great a cloud of witnesses, let us lay aside every weight, and the sin which so easily ensnares us, and let us run with endurance the race that is set before us, looking unto Jesus, the author and finisher of our faith, who for the **joy** that was set before Him endured the cross, despising the shame, and has sat down at the right hand of the throne of God. For consider Him who endured such hostility from sinners against Himself, lest you become weary and discouraged in your souls. HEBREWS 12:1-3*

Don't *ever* give up!

Sing praise to the LORD, you saints of His, And give thanks at the remembrance of His holy name. For His anger *is but for* a moment, His favor *is for* life; Weeping may endure for a night,

But **joy** *comes* in the morning. [6]Now in my prosperity I said, "I shall never be moved." Psalm 30: 4-6

PROLOGUE

This book includes everything you need to change your life today. My desire in writing it is to give you practical help to live an abundant life of liberty & true joy. Isn't it time to live your purpose? Picture yourself living a life full of freedom & joy! What would it look like for you? Write it down. Get detailed. Write out a plan.

If you would like help figuring out the 'HOW' I would be privileged to help. I'll COACH you and TRAIN you toward your NEW LIFE, LIBERTY and JOY. I will empower you to make more money, improve your relationships & enjoy better health so you can do all that God has called you to.

If you follow this book closely- basically, you'll be empowered to do whatever you want, whenever you want with whomever you want. After all, *true* wealth includes all of those things. You were born for this! Now go do it!

Made in the USA
Las Vegas, NV
30 June 2023